The Heart of a Woman

Lola Almanza

BookLeaf Publishing

The Heart of a Woman © 2022 Lola
Almanza

All rights reserved.

No part of this publication may be
reproduced, stored in a retrieval system, or
transmitted, in any form or by any means,
electronic, mechanical, photocopying,
recording or otherwise, without the prior
written permission of the presenters.

Lola Almanza asserts the moral right to be
identified as author of this work.

Presentation by *BookLeaf Publishing*

Web: www.bookleafpub.com

E-mail: info@bookleafpub.com

ISBN: 9789357744966

First edition 2022

I dedicate this book to my daughter Jocelyn and my son Derrek. May you always find hope and happiness within yourselves so that when love truly finds you, you are ready. And to my two best friends Sarah and Erica, who helped me through some of the tougher times I've grown from - you both mean the world to me.

ACKNOWLEDGEMENT

I was blessed with two of the best friends a girl could have while on this journey. Sarah Davis and Erica McClure. You've both been there for me through every tough road I've traveled over the last decade and I can't thank you enough for your support. You've both been a shoulder, confidant, and so much more. I sincerely appreciate you both.

I'd also like to thank my therapist for the encouragement in continuing my creative writing process. I'm sure not many see a therapist as I do, but I think it's important to mention her as she didn't just encourage, she supported and followed my healing journey acting a cheerleader, a teacher, and someone to help me really think through my feelings. In helping me process things, she's only helped to make my writing that much better.

PREFACE

When I started this project, I was going through a challenging time. After a divorce and a soon to be failed dating relationship, I took this challenge and decided to turn it into something positive. Something where I reflected on feelings from my divorce and from how I felt in the transition of leaving my most recent relationship. During the creative process I realized how much more love I had for myself and that sharing it in this way could only help others.

Love can be many things and in this book, I offer a glimpse into a writer s heart. One where the emotions of the heart take center stage and are not disregarded, but validated. Each piece offers a deep understanding through exploration of all the emotions we as humans feel where love is concerned. There is something in the telling of a story through poetry that can always uplift, help to connect, or inspire us.

You'll notice that some of the poetry in this book doesn't follow a simple rhyming pattern. Each one is different depending on where the creative process found me. A few are written with rhyming or as ballads while others are free verse.

From heartbreak, longing, feeling whole and complete, to feeling the brightest joy from the potential of true love, this collection of poetry is a true work from the heart. I hope that you enjoy it as much as I have enjoyed the writing process. I'm truly blessed to have been able to create them for you.

The breaking of a heart

The wind has ceased.
And time now stands still.
While I should be feeling unleashed,
Instead, I feel ill.

The breaking of a world,
A sacred vow...
The words now just sit uncurled.
In my heart disallowed.

As the tears fall
Through sleepless nights
And empty days without calls
The expectations sit in sleep.
Waiting for understanding that never comes.

When there are no longer words
Waiting to come out.
The tongue becomes a sword.
Slashing and thrashing all about.

It's the last defense.
To that which still remains broken.
The pain unhealed is immense.
But for how long will it remain unspoken?

Only time itself will tell.
Until then the feelings inside
Will ever more stay spelled.
Perhaps till they move aside or subside.

The Betrayal of Healing

Dirty work is the healing.
It's messy, uneven, and unrelenting.
There's no timeline.
There's no stars that magically align to give a
sign.
Somedays it feels great.
The leaving of a burden covered in an old band
aide.
And other days it's cruel.
As memories come crashing brutally through.
There are days of dark and of light.
But always, the sun is born after the night.
It is here in this place
Where we learn to accept and give grace
To ourselves as we accept and surrender
To the peace that leads to happiness in all its
splendor.
This is the place we strive to find each day.
Through the betrayal of healing in each and
every possible way.

After the Storm

Thunder strikes and crashes.
Rain pours and washes.
Hail beats a steady rhythm…
Like that of something breaking.
Similar to hearts beating out of sync.
Tears falling for that which is becoming more
lost with every passing moment.
Sitting, surrendering, being at peace and
knowing your own happiness is without.
Wishing joy could be again…
But that takes work.
Real love comes after the storms.
Commitment arising from two like the opposing
Sun and Moon.
There can be no light without dark.
And no dark without light.
Seeing hope with each new rise
Of the fiery ashes she is reborn.

The Wish and Gift of Loneliness

Letting all of the emotions flow
From within the deepest parts of your well
A solitude of peace grows.
A discovery of self-love dwells.

Using the connection to your deepest wishes
The only wish that matters you make.
It's not for the dirty to be made clean like dishes
It's for the most profound love to be had without
mistake.
And when the universe gives this gift
Oh, the elation, the hope, the joy it brings!

You work and pray each day it doesn't drift.
That nagging feeling of betrayal and
abandonment still rings...
Can it last or will self-sabotage win?
And this...
This is when the work truly begins.

To know yourself enough to see it for what it is.
Self-doubt not truly released.
Connection divided by the walls within

The work of loneliness not yet done becomes
increased.
And so, it begins again

Feeling all of that which you've always had.
Deep inside connected to it all.
The tiny tendrils of your self-love reaching out
like hands.
Not just for yourself, but to those you hold dear.

And to even those which have hurt you
This love you witness and bear it all.
The truth in that we are all connected.
Can it be true that loneliness is the key to
growing your own self love?
Is it not enough to know your self-worth?
To know that you deserve more.
Or is this a test to see if you have healed?

Perhaps this isn't a test, but a bigger question
One for which only your mind, body, heart, and
soul have the answer.
Is it worth it to stay in this place
Or would doing so leave you completely empty
-
A betrayal of your needs and wants.

Is this love enough to be patient.
To sit with it.

To surrender to it.
Only the wish of loneliness with time can tell.
Because you see, love can be maddening.
Not just in the best of ways, but also the worst.
It can be crippling and healing all at once.
So, to ask this question of a burdened heart
Oh, it's a lot...

When sacrifice is made will it be rewarded by
the loneliness in the end?
Will what feels hard now become so much more
in the end?
Like the temporary loss of the dying Phoenix,
There is always hope because it's destined to be
reborn.
Healed by tears.
Held by the grace of the wings of love.
This is the wish and gift of loneliness.

Honor & Presence

Reflecting on conversations.
Pausing only for ruminations.
I see the romantic side of you, of me, of us.
I see your light, joy, and love.
In everything you do to go above…
From the way you smile to the way you sigh
early in the morn.
In the depths of my own heart,
I know we won't be apart.
Yet, I still you miss you each moment of the day
when we are.
I want to honor all that you are.
Honor and be present for all that we are.
Together – where joy can't help but sing from
depths of my soul.

What You've Become

What you've become to me is something I didn't
think possible.
Someone I can naturally talk to about anything -
From my wildest desires, my random
ramblings, and everything between
These I can tell you without a care.
This makes you a great friend.
A best friend.

You've become more than just that though.
In a brief time, you became my romantic
partner.
Making all of time stand still as together we
ensure our pleasures together.
Exploring, igniting fire and passion, until in the
end
We are left breathless...
Oh, what an amazing romantic partner you are!

But beyond this, there is more.
A deep and intimate connection that made us
more than friends,
More than bed mates.
True partners in every sense of the word.

With daily communication even with distance
you've tried.
But here I sit asking for more.

To see you in person - to see you smile while
saying you love me.
I don't want just a phone call and memories of
our past.
I want a future where we can create more
memories together.
Where laughs can be had over the silliest of
things
And joy can be found in the simplest of notions
-
Like waking up next to you...

What you've become is so perplexing because
of where things are.
Will you ever have time for me again?
Will you ever see me in person again?
Why can't you say these things to me often to
reassure me you aren't pulling away?

So here I sit contemplating do I stay for

uncertainty or...
Do I go in hopes that I'm not losing who is truly
right for me?
In my heart I know what you've become to me.

In my soul I feel it, too.
Because what you've become and already were
Is so much more than I could have possibly
imagined.

It is in this space that while I can keep
pretending what we have is enough,
I know what you've truly become.
On different paths our feet trod growing further
and further apart.
With no means of seeing a possible future,
Here it ends with a sadness and understanding
that in this place…
There'll always be love, but not the kind that
allows for growth together.
There'll always be a fondness, but not
contentment.
In this place I wish you well and say goodbye to
what you were
And bless you for what you've now become.
A soon to be forgotten friend as we move
forward separately.

Between the Mind and Heart

When your mind says one thing,
Yet your heart says another,
Which is right?
The rational and unfeeling words that sting.
Or the emotional ones that feel shattered?
Healing is never overnight.
Those feelings that one feels,
They don't just go away.
They take time, patience, and self-love.
So endure for a short time the reels,
The dissonance between the two frays.
In the end, you'll rise above.
Take heart in your journey.
Always staying present
Just sitting with each emotion and letting it go.
Tomorrow isn't promised by any.
So live each moment with intent.
The heart and mind will soon follow.

Growing, Reflecting, and Sharing

Breathing deeply and just sitting.
Sitting with everything that you feel.
That's the path.
Not avoiding the pain and stirg,
Working through the hurt, angry, sad, and
surreal
That's where we can again learn to laugh.

Understanding that where we are and accepting
it.
This is where our own self-love grows.
Through this we find we are whole; complete.
It is in our own truth we commit
To love ourselves no matter life's flows.
Because without, we can't love others we meet.

When that self-love is examined and rebirthed
to its fullest potential,
Then you'll feel where your direction lies.
Not in the arms of another, but within yourself.
And then go and share what in life is so
essential –
Make your connections and look into their eyes.

So that you can see what is reflected from
within oneself.

Unbridled love, passion, and happiness.
These are the keys to what you seek.
And to what you already have within.
Then manifest that which you desire and
process.
Every single day, even when feeling meek.
Just go out and share it all as a beautiful song
played on a violin.

Expectations

What are these things taking up space?
Ideas, fantasies, and misguided notions.
None that in the end offer solace.
That is what they are – expectations.

Cast them aside.
Make the room for all that you desire.
Keep your boundaries, stay for the ride.
Dance to the music and see what transpires.

Be ok with feeling it all.
The anxious excitement, nervousness, and
unsureness.
Let it all in and flow away like the cascading
waterfall.
The emotions healing like water as before they
leave, they caress.

Accept where you are in this very moment.
Feel your strength, your grace, your love.
Know that its here, your truth is transparent.
You can and do begin again.

You've made room because you've simply let
go.

Expectations no longer needed or wanted.
The desires to manifest you chose are thorough.
The space is there for your true beloved.

Something New

It's ok to remember those kind, sweet
memories.
It's ok to remember those feelings from those
moments.
They don't define you or your trajectory.
They are part of your past growth and
self-investment.

It's ok to move on and think forward.
Staying present in each minute is a gift.
A blessing to help you to grow inward.
A place in time that can uplift.

So, take the chance and live fully.
Breathe in all that you're feeling.
Sing with passion oh so loudly.
Your song of love and longing.

Let them be the cause of your laughter.
Let them see you smile and be joyful.
Be there as you would for your daughter.
Be there as much as you are beautiful.

Take your time.
Your heart will know who.
This magical find.
Something new.

The Dance

When the song that fills you with hope plays
Let it fill you and breathe in all the good.
Feel it so deeply you can't help but move.
Every fiber of your being knows it to be true.
The excitement, anticipation, and joy of life.
It finds you whole and full of love.

This is the dance.
The one where you open your heart.
You feel the expansion within you
All the work you've been doing.
It's finally paid off as you feel it all.

It doesn't matter if you feel anxious or nervous,
Just feel it and let your body do what it knows
best.
Because this?
This is the stuff that magic is made from.

The choices you've made up until now.
They make you, you.
And that makes this so much sweeter.
So, enjoy the ride.
Enjoy the blissful dance.
Hold it close to you as fondly as you can.

But allow it to grow, to flourish.
To become what it will.

The most special moments you'll always have.
The future is unwritten, a blank page.
Fill it with love, joy, hope, and patience.
And remember to dance.

Reflection

Sometimes we see what we want.
The things we want so much that our eyes lose true focus.
We can even tell ourselves we feel a certain way.
When under the surface, there is doubt.

But turning to our own blind eye.
We ignore the truth.
Because of what we want to see reflected.

Smoke and mirrors are the game.
Truth is not in their nature.
Yet it always finds us.
Shedding light on the reflection of what we thought we wanted.
What we thought we saw, heard, felt, and even believed.

The feeling of not really being connected...
That. That was the truth.
The feeling of not really being wanted.
That was truth, too.
Because when as humans we truly and deeply want something,

We do everything in our power to make that
happen.

This is why it's so easy see what we want.
Rather than the truth we know intuitively.
Instinctively.
To see something through the smoke and
mirrors other than truth.
That is just the game of false reflection.

Here I sit.
Finally at peace.
Moving forward and feeling whole, complete,
And truly grounded in my own truth.
Now I see my reflection.

I know what I want,
But I also know that I can't allow someone else
to do my work
Let alone be something they are truly not.
Accepting what was and allowing it to pass,

I make room for me, my wants, my desires, my
everything.
The potential of what could be will be.
And when it is, I'll know it deeply to the roots
of my being.

It won't just be a reflection of my wants and
desires.
It will be honest, true, pure, and raw.
Even in its most filtered light it will be real.

The Choice To Love

They say love always finds a way.
That the heart will know when it knows.
And what does my heart know?

It knows that now,
In this space and moment
I am safe, I am loved.
I can choose to love and offer safety to those I
choose.

But what is love?
A mixture of chemicals turned cocktail in our
body?
Or a choice we make to endure it all…
For that special person that we choose.

Could it be more than that?
Perhaps a bright and deep connection to
someone?
One that leads us to choose them over others.
Or perhaps it's simply fate.

All we can know is that when it's right,
We will truly know.
Not within one day, week, or month.

But within a singular moment when everything
 stops.

When the world stands still.
And all we see in our mind, body, and soul
Is this person whom we truly know,
Feels the same without saying it.

This. This is the choice we get to make.
In this moment we get to choose that person.
We get to open ourselves to every possible
future –
One where love just isn't fanned, but
strengthened, grown, and most of all,
Chosen.
This is the choice to love.

Taking a Chance

We talk on the way to that place.
Our first meeting place; a date.
Something lighthearted, easy, fun.
Arriving at the same time, we see each other.
Saying hello we embrace the other as if we
know each other well.

He's sweet, anxious, and somewhat charming.
The conversation is easy and dining together…
It's comfortable like we've known each other
for more than just this meeting.
His eyes draw me in as does his smile.

The witty remarks are pleasant and humorous.
He's trying, but he's not.
He's not driving the conversation and yet,
Neither am I.
It's refreshing with no agenda.
No expectations.

Seated for hours we begin to leave.
Making plans for a trip to a park to get some
exercise and enjoy the weather.
And then…
He kisses me ever so gently.

A first to remember of all firsts.
He took a chance and so did I.

After we part, already I feel blessed.
To take this chance.
To allow things to flow effortlessly.
To be present.
To allow a connection that feels natural –
Not rushed or forced.

After a few more meetings together already I've
decided.
This is the best chance I could've taken.
Still is my heart, my soul.
Completely at peace and safe.
I'm whole without him, but the joy that exists
with him is beautiful.

Grounded in my truth at the deepest recesses of
my core.
I know who I am and it's not what I was told
before.
I'm more confident and secure now.
Enough to know that regardless of the path
we're on,
Together, we are taking a chance.

Just Have Fun

Giddy, maybe nervous or anxious.
All to see him.
We're just having fun and getting to know each
other.
That's what I keep saying out loud to everyone.
I'm only seeing him on my way home this
evening.
Maybe it's because wearing a dress is out of my
element?
Or maybe it's because I want him to see me
dressed my best.

Sigh. All these feelings.
Take it slow. Breathe.
Let things play out.
Really get to know him and remember to reflect
each day.
Ask yourself the hard questions after each day.
Know that you don't need this because you
 don't.
These are things I hear internally.

Reflecting on every relationship prior.
Looking at positives and negatives.
Seeing where the valuable lessons are.

Ensuring I don't overlook something that will
 truly bother me later.
Later, when the excitement has worn off.

For now, I'll just enjoy the feelings.
I'll have fun and be safe.
I'll not rush the important things.
I'll flirt and stay sweet, sassy, and sarcastic.
I'll promise myself to be as authentic and true
to myself as possible.
Because I want to be sure he sees me for me –
raw and unfiltered.
While at other times refined and professional.

I want to know these things from him as well.
What's his greatest fear?
Does he have regrets?
What about his proudest accomplishment?
His greatest passion?
I want to know it all before I make a choice –
To stay or go.

But for now, I only know this.
I'm at peace within myself.
Grounded firmly in my truth and yet,
I'm still able to feel all of these surprising
feelings.
So again, I'll remember that I'm just having fun
getting to know him.

Connection

Connecting in a once in a lifetime moment.
Breathing deeply and feeling into our cores.
It's easy to say "I,' but really it is we.
We, us, together joined by mother nature.
With her majestic views, her patience, her
 gentle caress as the wind blows.
Deeply grounded in this one moment.
Forever to be remembered as something so
intimate
Without ever so much as touching.
This is true connection.

When we can't wait to wake up and say good
morning
Or miss the other so much that even a short text
sends a feeling of joy through the other's spine.
All because we know they're thinking about us
 and miss us.
When we don't want to say goodnight but know
that we must.
And so, again we look forward to our next
phone call to hear the other's voice.
Is this what being connected to someone feels
like?

When your heart sings thinking about stolen
moments.
It sometimes skips a beat because you are one
moment closer.
Closer to the time you can hold each other safe
from the rest of the world.
When you can look into each other's eyes and
just know.
With every fiber of your being.
This. This is feeling connected.

There's no need for over indulgent words.
Those that end up being unfelt, unreal, rushed,
or forced.
Just getting to be present and feel whatever
comes.
It's a safe place to hold our heads on the other's
chest.
To be there in a way that no one else can.
This deep connection allows for such a
beautiful space.

Flowing as gently and easy as the river
We move in time while taking in every single
moment.
Together we both feel at ease.
Knowing that each day is a gift to be cherished.
Caring for ourselves first but never forgetting or
disregarding the other…

Our bond is so deep that even the vast ocean couldn't break what it is.
A connection we've both hoped for that isn't just a dream.

Loving Myself

The first time I heard this phrase,
I knew what it was, but not really what it meant.
It was said in haste from another.
One who was right, but not for me.
You need to love yourself first…
I thought I did.

I was proud of my accomplishments,
My courage to grow through adversity,
My strength to carry on as a mother alone,
My beauty, intellect, all of it.
I thought I loved myself.

In hindsight, I did, but not really.
Had I truly loved myself, oh how different
things would've been.
I would've left long ago.
Never settled or accepted what I was told.
I should've listened to my feelings telling me…
He wasn't the one.
And I; I needed to love myself enough to leave
the relationship.

Now after truly removing the blinders I can see
where I didn't.

Being able to look at things and know I am
complete –
That a partner isn't needed for me to feel
fulfilled.
I am worthy.
I am beautiful.
I am intelligent.
I am talented.
I am so much more and
I am loved.

Do I have everything I want?
No, but I am happy. I am safe.
I have balance, confidence.
Most of all, I've accepted every aspect of
myself.
Even the hardest parts of myself.
This.
This is loving myself.

The Colors of Healing

Blue isn't the color of sadness.
It's one of intuition, imagination, and freedom.
Red isn't just the color of our blood or heart.
It's one of love, passion, and energetic action.
Yellow isn't a color for yielding to others.
This color is one of hope, light, and all that is
good like the rising sun.
Green, unlike others isn't just the color of grass
that grounds us.
It's representative of growth, abundance, and
the possibility of what we speak.
Purple isn't just the color of a pretty stone or
royalty.
This is all about healing, being devoted to self
and others, and of course believing in the magic
of life.
So, breathe it all in – every ounce of it.
Define yourself and create your own color
 palate.
Describe who you are and who you want to be
in every sense of the colored strokes you brush.
Although yesterday is completed tomorrow is a
brush stroke away.
Paint it well with the colors of healing you
choose.

The Rising Phoenix

The ashes are mourned.
Happiness subsides and hurt reigns.
Emerging through the darkest of nights.

Rough roads less traveled and hard work to do.
Intellect won't work or help in this place.
Shiny things only reflect the loss.
In this night, there is the faintest glimpse of
light.
Now drawing closer, the self begins to
recognize it.
Giving yourself what you need, you find
strength.

Placating ends and love become the bridge to
your growth.
Happiness is hinted, just beyond the layers of
ash.
Opening the heart to self-love,
Ever after is a reality and a place of endless
possibility.
No longer doubting the strength you carry,
Igniting your love, passion, and all that you are,
 you rise.

X-rays aren't needed to see the beautiful
Phoenix you are as you rise again.